Porcupine

Christine Webster

www.av2books.com

Step 1
Go to **www.av2books.com**

Step 2
Enter this unique code

PMBJTVMTI

Step 3
Explore your interactive eBook!

CONTENTS

AV2 is optimized for use on any device

Your interactive eBook comes with...

Contents
Browse a live contents page to easily navigate through resources

Audio
Listen to sections of the book read aloud

Videos
Watch informative video clips

Weblinks
Gain additional information for research

Try This!
Complete activities and hands-on experiments

Key Words
Study vocabulary, and complete a matching word activity

Quizzes
Test your knowledge

Slideshows
View images and captions

... and much, much more!

Contents

Meet the Porcupine

A porcupine is a plump animal with a round head and thick coat. Porcupines are best known for the long, pointed spikes growing from their back and sides. These are called quills. They are sharp like needles.

Porcupines use their quills to stay safe from **predators**. If a porcupine is threatened, muscles in its skin make the quills stand up on end. The porcupine then sticks some of its quills into the predator's skin.

Porcupines are great swimmers. Although the tips of their quills are solid, the shafts are hollow. This helps the animals float.

A porcupine can have
as many as 30,000
quills. Each quill has a
sharp tip on the end.

Where Porcupines Live

There are approximately two dozen **species** of porcupines on Earth. These **rodents** have a variety of **habitats**. They live in forests, deserts, and grasslands.

Porcupines belong to two main groups. These are Old World porcupines and New World porcupines. Old World porcupines are found in Europe, Africa, and Asia. New World porcupines live in forests and wooded areas in North, Central, and South America.

The Mexican hairy dwarf porcupine can be found from Mexico to Panama.

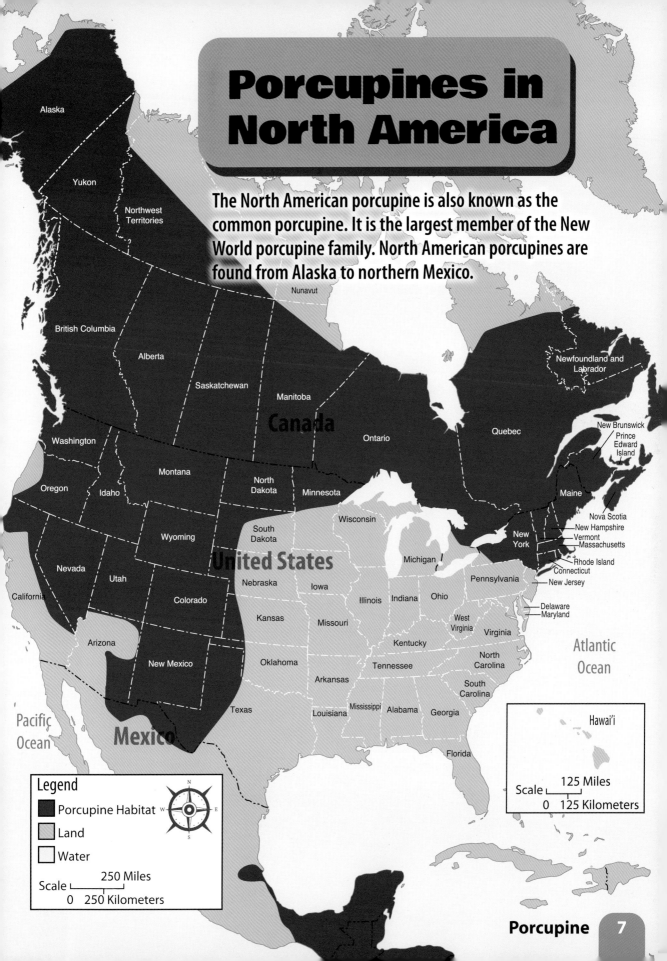

Porcupines in North America

The North American porcupine is also known as the common porcupine. It is the largest member of the New World porcupine family. North American porcupines are found from Alaska to northern Mexico.

Alaska

Yukon

Northwest Territories

Nunavut

British Columbia

Alberta

Saskatchewan

Manitoba

Newfoundland and Labrador

Canada

Ontario

Quebec

New Brunswick

Prince Edward Island

Washington

Montana

North Dakota

Minnesota

Maine

Oregon

Idaho

Wisconsin

Nova Scotia

New Hampshire

Vermont

Massachusetts

Wyoming

South Dakota

Michigan

New York

Rhode Island

Connecticut

New Jersey

United States

Nevada

Utah

Nebraska

Iowa

Pennsylvania

Delaware

Maryland

California

Colorado

Kansas

Missouri

Illinois

Indiana

Ohio

West Virginia

Virginia

Atlantic Ocean

Arizona

Kentucky

New Mexico

Oklahoma

Tennessee

North Carolina

Arkansas

South Carolina

Pacific Ocean

Texas

Louisiana

Mississippi

Alabama

Georgia

Mexico

Florida

Hawai'i

Scale

125 Miles

0   125 Kilometers

Legend

■ Porcupine Habitat

☐ Land

☐ Water

Scale

250 Miles

0   250 Kilometers

Porcupine History

No one knows for certain how long porcupines have been on Earth. There are few **fossils** to tell us about their **ancestors**. Scientists think that porcupines came from South America to North America about 3 million years ago.

In the 1800s and 1900s, many settlers trapped beavers and **fishers** for their fur. Fishers often **prey** on porcupines. With fewer fishers to hunt them, porcupine populations grew very large. People were paid to hunt porcupines to stop the animals from harming forests.

The word *porcupine* comes from a French term, porc d'épine. This means "thorny pork."

Early North American settlers called the porcupine the quill pig because it reminded them of a wild pig with spines.

Porcupine Shelter

Porcupines search for hollow spaces to sleep inside. Their homes are called dens. Most times, a porcupine sleeps alone. It may sleep in a den with another porcupine in winter.

Porcupines prefer to live in shady places. They also look for areas that are safe from predators. These include caves, hollow fallen trees, snowbanks, tree branches, or rocky places. Sometimes, they crawl under a deck or inside a shed.

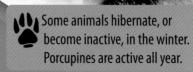
Some animals hibernate, or become inactive, in the winter. Porcupines are active all year.

Porcupines live in an area of about 25 to 35 acres (10 to 14 hectares). This is called their home range.

Porcupine Features

Porcupines are round and chubby. They have long, brownish-yellow to black fur. The fur looks soft, but it is covered in **barbed** quills.

FEET AND LEGS
Porcupines have a slow, waddling walk and strong feet for climbing trees. The rough soles of their feet have no hair. Their legs are short, but sturdy.

TAIL
Some porcupines have a strong tail. It can grasp objects. Porcupines use their tail to climb trees.

QUILLS

Quills are found on the porcupine's back and sides. Some porcupines also have quills on their head and tail. The quills are longest on the **rump**.

HEAD

Porcupines have a small head and ears, and almost no neck. Their eyes are small. These animals do not see well, but their senses of hearing and smell are very strong.

TEETH

Porcupines have bright orange teeth. Their teeth are strong. The **incisors** never stop growing. Porcupines use their teeth to chew tough wood and seeds.

What Do Porcupines Eat?

Porcupines are herbivores. This means they do not eat meat. Tree bark is their main food source. Porcupines eat about 1 pound (0.5 kilograms) of plant matter each day.

Porcupines chew through the outer bark to get to the **cambium**. This is the main source of their diet in the winter. During the winter, they also feed on twigs, pine needles, and branches. In the summer, porcupines eat leaves, grass, roots, berries, stems, fruits, seeds, flowers, and nuts.

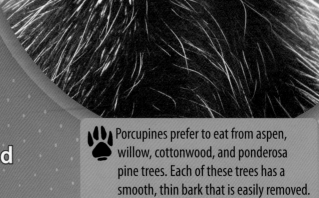

Porcupines prefer to eat from aspen, willow, cottonwood, and ponderosa pine trees. Each of these trees has a smooth, thin bark that is easily removed.

Porcupines grunt when they look for food.

Porcupine Life Cycle

Porcupines mate at the end of summer and in early fall. A female begins **breeding** when she is between 12 and 18 months old. Often, males are about 2 years old when they begin to breed.

Babies

Baby porcupines, or porcupettes, are born about seven months after the male and female mate. The porcupette's quills are soft at birth. Within hours, they harden. After a few days, the porcupette will begin to look for food.

Mature

Young female porcupines leave their mothers when they are about 6 months of age. Males remain nearby. In nature, porcupines live for about 15 years.

A female porcupine uses high-pitched sounds to **attract** a male. Often, more than one male responds. The males then compete for the female. Sometimes, they will even fight. The winning male does a special dance and makes a series of grunts.

4 to 5 Months Old

Porcupines often have only one porcupette. It drinks milk from its mother for about four to five months. During this time, it learns where to find food and how to protect itself.

Encountering Porcupines

Many porcupines enjoy the taste of salt. They will chew wooden tools to taste the salty sweat left behind on the handles. Porcupines also eat salt used to melt ice on roads. Often, people will put out salt blocks for porcupines to lick.

Porcupines are not **aggressive** animals. They are slow-moving and only use their quills to protect themselves against predators. If you see a porcupine in nature, it is best to stay away.

Porcupines stamp their back feet when they feel threatened.

Many people think porcupines are pests. This is because they kill trees by eating their bark.

Myths and Legends

There are many myths about porcupines. At one time, people thought that porcupines could shoot their quills through the air. This is not true.

A porcupine turns its back to a nearby predator as a warning. If the predator does not leave, the porcupine may shake its body. This may loosen some quills, making it look as though they are shooting out at the predator.

 Some Native Americans use porcupine quills to decorate clothing, moccasins, birchbark boxes, and pouches.

How Porcupine Got His Quills

The Chippewa have a legend explaining why porcupines have quills. One day, Bear saw Porcupine and wanted to eat him. Porcupine climbed to the top of a tree to protect himself. The next day, Porcupine sat under a hawthorn tree. The thorns on the tree pricked him. This gave Porcupine an idea. He broke off the branches and put them on his back. Then, he went into the woods to wait for Bear.

When Bear jumped at Porcupine, he curled into a ball, and the thorns pricked Bear. A spirit named Nanabozho wanted to help Porcupine. He took more branches from the hawthorn tree and peeled off the bark. Then, he used clay to stick the branches to Porcupine's back. They became part of Porcupine's body. When Wolf jumped on Porcupine, he ran away crying. Then, Bear came along, but he avoided Porcupine. This is why all porcupines have quills today.

Quiz

1 What are the two types of porcupines?

2 How long do porcupines live in nature?

3 Why are porcupines good swimmers?

4 What are porcupines' homes called?

5 Why are porcupines considered pests?

6 How many quills can a porcupine have?

7 According to Chippewa legend, which spirit gave porcupines their quills?

8 What are baby porcupines called?

Key Words

aggressive: likely to attack

ancestors: people, plants, objects, or animals from the past

attract: cause to come to a place

barbed: having a sharp point that curves backwards

breeding: mating to produce babies

cambium: a delicate layer of tissue between the inner bark and the wood of a tree

fishers: a type of weasel

fossils: traces of an animal that are left behind in rocks

habitats: the places where animals live

incisors: front teeth used for cutting and gnawing

predators: animals that hunt other animals for food

prey: to hunt and kill for food

rodents: gnawing mammals that are distinguished by strong, constantly growing incisors, and no canine teeth

rump: the back end of the body

species: animals or plants that share certain features and can breed together

Index

Get the best of both worlds.

AV2 bridges the gap between print and digital.

The expandable resources toolbar enables quick access to content including **videos**, **audio**, **activities**, **weblinks**, **slideshows**, **quizzes**, and **key words**.

Animated videos make static images come alive.

Resource icons on each page help readers to further **explore key concepts**.

Published by AV2
350 5th Avenue, 59th Floor
New York, NY   10118
Website: www.av2books.com

Library of Congress Control Number: 2019955128
ISBN 978-1-7911-2095-5 (hardcover)
ISBN 978-1-7911-2096-2 (softcover)
ISBN 978-1-7911-2097-9 (multi-user eBook)
ISBN 978-1-7911-2098-6 (single-user eBook)

Printed in Guangzhou, China
1 2 3 4 5 6 7 8 9 0 24 23 22 21 20

022020
101119

Editor: Katie Gillespie
Designer: Ana María Vidal

Every reasonable effort has been made to trace ownership and to obtain permission to reprint copyright material. The publishers would be pleased to have any errors or omissions brought to their attention so that they may be corrected in subsequent printings.

AV2 acknowledges Getty Images, Alamy, Minden Pictures, iStock, and Shutterstock as its primary image suppliers for this title.